The Call of Ephesians

Building the Church of Today

The Call of Ephesians

Building the Church of Today

Tim R. Barker, D. Min.

Superintendent of the South Texas
District of the Assemblies of God

Tim R. Barker Ministries

THE CALL OF EPHESIANS: BUILDING THE CHURCH OF TODAY,
Barker, Tim.
1st ed.

Formatting, proofing, and cover provided by:
Farley Dunn of

 THREE SKILLET

www.ThreeSkilletPublishing.com

Scripture passages are from The Holy Bible, New International Version®
(NIV®), copyright © 1973, 1978, 1984, 2011 by Biblica, Inc.™ All rights
reserved. Used by permission of Zondervan.

ISBN: 978-1-7346669-9-1

Dedication

Danny Alexander, Ph.D., and
Amy Alexander, Ph.D.

You believed I could do this.

Thank you.

Contents

Preface

Acknowledgements

Introduction

Preface

The concept for this book started with a series of sermons on the book of Ephesians.

Ephesians is divided into two clear segments. First, Paul presents the truths that form the foundation of a Christian life. Second, Paul shows us how these truths enable us to live out our commitment to God as a holy community of dedicated believers.

It's only when we live out the truths of Christ that we become a testimony to the lost that will draw them to Christ.

Paul understood that legalism can become a hindrance to our Christian walk and that we must focus on Christ and Christ alone. When our faith hits the road, God is there with us. He challenges us to trust Him to walk at our side through every challenge we might face.

That's Paul's message in a nutshell, and it's vital we take it to heart.

Acknowledgements

Dr. Adonna Otwell at Southwestern Assemblies of God University was instrumental in my schooling and future success in my ministry.

Thank you, Dr. Otwell, for your trust, faith, and belief that I could reach the heights that God had in mind for me.

The Call of Ephesians

Building the Church of Today

Introduction

Paul of the New Testament is the ultimate example of what God's salvation power can do to take a sinner and turn their life around.

This book is a plan to enable you to become a Paul – *a power Christian* – someone able to build a better Church and fight the warfare that is our Christian walk in the 21st century.

Consider this your manual and training guide. That's certainly what Ephesians is. In the pages of this book, I've tried to expound on and clarify Paul's intent. His words were applicable to the 1st century Christians, and they will equip the modern-day Church to march to victory against Satan and his evil minions.

Get set. Ready your armor. The war is on, and you are being asked to fight.

Tim Barker, Superintendent
South Texas District Assemblies of God
February 2020

The Church Is the Body of Christ.

For he chose us in him before the creation of the world to be holy and blameless in his sight. In love he predestined us for adoption to sonship through Jesus Christ ...

~Paul~

Ephesians
Chapter One

THE CHURCH

~ *Chapter One* ~

A BODY

Ephesians 1:1-23

*Paul, an apostle of Christ Jesus by the will
of God,*

*To God's holy people in Ephesus, the
faithful in Christ Jesus:*

*Grace and peace to you from God our
Father and the Lord Jesus Christ.*

*Praise be to the God and Father of our
Lord Jesus Christ, who has blessed us in*

the heavenly realms with every spiritual blessing in Christ. For he chose us in him before the creation of the world to be holy and blameless in his sight. In love he predestined us for adoption to sonship through Jesus Christ, in accordance with his pleasure and will—to the praise of his glorious grace, which he has freely given us in the One he loves. In him we have redemption through his blood, the forgiveness of sins, in accordance with the riches of God's grace that he lavished on us. With all wisdom and understanding, he made known to us the mystery of his will according to his good pleasure, which he purposed in Christ, to be put into effect when the times reach their fulfillment—to bring unity to all things in heaven and on earth under Christ.

In him we were also chosen, having been predestined according to the plan of him who works out everything in conformity with the purpose of his will, in order that we, who were the first to put our hope in Christ, might be for the praise of his glory. And you also were included in Christ when you heard the message of truth, the gospel of your salvation. When you believed, you were marked in him with a seal, the promised Holy Spirit, who is a deposit guaranteeing our inheritance until the redemption of those who are God's possession—to the praise of his glory.

For this reason, ever since I heard about your faith in the Lord Jesus and your love for all God's people, I have not stopped giving thanks for you, remembering you in my prayers. I keep asking that the God of our Lord Jesus Christ, the glorious Father, may give you the Spirit of wisdom and revelation, so that you may know him better. I pray that the eyes of your heart may be enlightened in order that you may know the hope to which he has called you, the riches of his glorious inheritance in his holy people, and his incomparably great power for us who believe. That power is the same as the mighty strength he exerted when he raised Christ from the dead and seated him at his right hand in the heavenly realms, far above all rule and authority, power and dominion, and every name that is invoked, not only in the present age but also in the one to come.

*And God placed all things under his feet
and appointed him to be head over
everything for the church, which is his
body, the fullness of him who fills
everything in every way.*

Ephesians Is the Exception

While many of the New Testament books were written to assist the Church in problem solving, Ephesians is the exception. It also doesn't address heresy or errors as some of the other writings of Paul. However, he did wish to have the early Church understand her purpose, her power, her place in God's purposes and plans.

Paul explains the nature and call of the Church through six images in this book:

1. The Church – A Body
2. The Church – A Temple
3. The Church – A Mystery
4. The Church – A New Man
5. The Church – A Bride
6. The Church – A Soldier

In this book, we will examine the nature of the Church as God intended it to be. We will marvel in each image at what God has planned for His Church and rejoice over the ultimate victory that is assured.

How the World Sees the Church

The world sees the Church as an ineffective, weak, out-of-date organization that contributes little or nothing to society as a whole. This is in direct contrast with the Bible which portrays the Church as the powerful enemy of Satan, and as the agent of truth in a world of moral uncertainty. Satan himself cannot kill the Church of Jesus Christ, and the Church is what holds back the powers of evil from being fully unleashed in this world today. We must stand tall and not allow the world to trivialize the presence of the Church in this world. Remember, we are the expressed plan of God until He comes again!

The Church Is About Christ

The Church is Christ's body in the world ... this is an amazing reality. The Church is not just about us, it is about Christ!

The Bible teaches us that the Church is the power of God in the world today. The Church must not allow anything to divide it, destroy it, nor deprecate it … it is the only organization on earth that will triumph in the end!

God's Plan for the Church

God had planned the existence of the Church from the beginning of time! As His body, He has planned for us to be blameless and holy. The Church is not so much a building as it is a body! Unlike some religions that have sacred buildings, Christianity has no particular building that represents the "Church" … because the Church is a body and not a building! The Church is not made up of perfect people, but forgiven people. This is what makes us holy and blameless! This is an important difference! Therefore, we learn to love each other and see each other as Christ sees us, not as we are in the flesh, but what we are in the Spirit!

It's been said that anyone can love the ideal Church. The challenge is to love the real Church.

The Evidence of a Supernatural Church

One of the greatest evidences that the Church is a supernatural agency is the fact that it keeps surviving in spite of governmental systems, economic crisis, moral collapses, and world wars ... especially since it is made up of flawed people! What else explains its survival through thousands of years? What else explains its survival through all kinds of political systems? What else explains its survival through all kinds of economic situations?

The Church Cannot Fail

God planned for the Church's existence ... to be the representation of His body on earth ... therefore it will not fail. Not even the gates of Hell will prevail against it. Just as Hell failed to destroy the body of Christ after the cross, so it will fail to destroy the body of Christ as the Church! In this we cannot boast ... only in Christ can we boast, for He keeps His body alive and well! If you want to be a part of something that will survive until the end of time, join the Church, Christ's body! The Church will be here long after the present nations of this earth have disappeared! You can't lose being joined with Christ!

Paul says that Christ has:

"... lavished on us with all wisdom and understanding." (v. 8)

The Secret of the Church's Survival

The Church's strength and survival is a mystery to the world! Christ's cleansing power from sin is what joins us together, not our systems of government, not our fancy structures, not our programs. It is Christ's forgiveness! You can't get this in the world!

A leading British humanist was once interviewed and in a moment of surprising candor, she said, "What I envy most about you Christians is your forgiveness. I have nobody to forgive me."

It was by believing that we were:

"... marked in Him with a seal, the promised Holy Spirit." (v. 13b)

We Are Joined as One Body Through Forgiveness in Christ

This is what joins us together as the body of Christ: our forgiveness and God's grace through faith in Christ. Too many people in the Church forget this, and they get hung up on petty issues instead. We must allow the cleansing power of the

Holy Spirit to unite us ... this is the idea of the image of a "BODY" for the Church ... a body works together though there are different parts. A body has many parts but is one unit. Each part has a unique function, but always to benefit the whole and not just itself. Any Church where one member is working against another is not a fit body of Christ!!!

We Are United in Grace and Forgiveness

It is the grace and forgiveness of Christ that unites us as a whole. We share in His divine life and strength together so that we are built up as a whole! We are united together as one by His Spirit, not by our talents or abilities. We must never lose sight of what joins us together. If our unity is based on anything else but Christ's grace and cleansing power, no matter how important it seems to the world, it will not hold!

Prayer Provides Unity!

What helps keep this unity of Spirit? PRAYER for and with one another!

Paul often had to deal with a sick Church body, brothers fighting brothers, or sisters at war with sisters (as in Euodia and Syntyche[1] in Phil. 4).

In all his dealings with Church problems however, prayer was a basic foundation, and he was quick to mention it in regard to every Church and situation. Prayer helps keep the body healthy and helps keep each part sensitive to the other parts of the body. This is necessary to help it function properly. This is necessary to heal the wounds. This is necessary to harness the power of the parts together.

Prayer Helps the Church Function!

Prayer brings together the differing parts of the Church body so they can function as a whole! It helps keep proper perspective and love flowing. It helps keep a proper focus on God and not self. Prayer was never an afterthought for Paul. It was a basic element of his love and concern for the Church. Hence he says in Ephesians 1:16-17a:

"I have not stopped giving thanks for you,

---

[1] Euodia and Syntyche were part of the Church in Philippi who had "contended at [Paul's] side in the cause of the gospel" (Phil. 4:3). According to the book of Ephesians, they were involved in a disagreement (The Word doesn't say what.) and Paul felt it was his duty to resolve the disagreement for the betterment of the Church as a whole and as an example for Christian unity.

*remembering you in my prayers. I keep
asking that the God of our Lord Jesus
Christ..."*

The underlining is mine to illustrate this question: *How often do you pray for the Church? For your Church body?* There would be less division in Churches if more people prayed for one another!

Prayer Is Power!

The Church is not powerless in this world! Too often the Church acts like it is impotent against the world. We are almost apologetic for our existence. We must be careful not to have a siege mentality! Many times, we have heard it said that the Church is surrounded by an evil and hostile world, like a besieged fortress. We need to remember that it is also true that the Church is surrounded by God's love and care! Individually and collectively, we are blanketed by God's love as the earth is blanketed by the atmosphere. God loves the Church and will never forsake her.

The Source of Prayer's Power

Our power in the Church doesn't come from clever programs, nor institutional shrewdness, nor political strength ... it comes from the Gospel of Jesus Christ! We can offer EVERYONE in the world a real change of heart! We can show the world that Christ DOES make a difference. We can teach the world the REAL truth about life. We must not shrink away or be intimidated, for we have the power of God unto salvation in the Gospel of Jesus Christ! If we don't share the truth of salvation with this world, who will? We must be careful to recognize the difference between being culturally relevant and Christianity compromised!

Longing for a Historical Faith

I heard it said this way: As the Church today gets more and more hip – more and more need-oriented, responding to the buttons that people push in their pews – I find myself longing for more of a historical faith. I find myself not wanting to have everything explained to me in simple terms. I'm not even sure I want all my needs met as much as I want to meet God, and sometimes I wonder if He's really interested in the noise of our contemporary clamoring. Like my dog who can't seem to get anywhere because he keeps having to stop and scratch his fleas, I wonder if we are so busy scratching where everybody itches that we aren't taking anyone anywhere significant.

Revelation, Edification, Consecration!

Where does the Church's power come from? Our power doesn't come from <u>relevance</u>, it comes from <u>revelation</u>! Our power doesn't come from <u>entertainment</u>, it comes from <u>edification</u>! Our power doesn't come from <u>structures</u>, it comes from <u>scripture</u>! Our power doesn't come from <u>programs</u>, it comes from <u>prayer</u>! Our power doesn't come from <u>cash</u>, it comes from <u>cleansing</u> and <u>consecration</u>!

The verses in Ephesians 1:18-19 are especially important:

> *"I pray also that the eyes of your heart*
> *may be <u>enlightened</u> in order that you may*
> *know the hope to which he has called you,*
> *the riches of his glorious inheritance in the*
> *saints, and his incomparably great power*
> *for us who believe. That power is like the*
> *working of his mighty strength ..."*

The Church Is ONE BODY

The Church must stand tall, avoid schisms that weaken it, and stand as ONE body filled with the power of the Holy Spirit in a world that desperately needs the message of the Gospel! We must function as a whole. We must be united. We will be victorious. The Church is Christ's body and will be triumphant because Christ is the head of His body, not a man! As a body we act in this world to express the works of God, that of forgiveness, healing, helping, and courage. When Christ's body acts as a united body, Satan cannot stand against it! The greatest power in this world is not a government, it is God's body!

Called! Unified! Empowered!

The image of the Church as THE body of Christ was meant to emphasize the function and unity of the Church. We are "one" body – created to work together in unity. Christ's body should not be divided. Believers are joined together by Christ's love and sacrifice. We are called to work together and to love each other despite all our weaknesses and differences. We are Christ's body and can dramatically affect the world around us!

The Church Is a Temple to the Lord.

And in him you too are being built together to become a dwelling in which God lives by his Spirit.

~Paul~

Ephesians
Chapter Two

— *Chapter Two* —

A TEMPLE

Ephesians 2:1-22

As for you, you were dead in your transgressions and sins, in which you used to live when you followed the ways of this world and of the ruler of the kingdom of the air, the spirit who is now at work in those who are disobedient. All of us also lived among them at one time, gratifying the cravings of our flesh and following its desires and thoughts. Like the rest, we were by nature deserving of wrath. But because of his great love for us, God, who

*is rich in mercy, made us alive with Christ
even when we were dead in
transgressions—it is by grace you have
been saved. And God raised us up with
Christ and seated us with him in the
heavenly realms in Christ Jesus, in order
that in the coming ages he might show the
incomparable riches of his grace,
expressed in his kindness to us in Christ
Jesus. For it is by grace you have been
saved, through faith—and this is not from
yourselves, it is the gift of God—not by
works, so that no one can boast. For we
are God's handiwork, created in Christ
Jesus to do good works, which God
prepared in advance for us to do.*

*Therefore, remember that formerly you
who are Gentiles by birth and called
"uncircumcised" by those who call
themselves "the circumcision" (which is
done in the body by human hands)—
remember that at that time you were
separate from Christ, excluded from
citizenship in Israel and foreigners to the
covenants of the promise, without hope
and without God in the world. But now in
Christ Jesus you who once were far away*

have been brought near by the blood of Christ.

For he himself is our peace, who has made the two groups one and has destroyed the barrier, the dividing wall of hostility, by setting aside in his flesh the law with its commands and regulations. His purpose was to create in himself one new humanity out of the two, thus making peace, and in one body to reconcile both of them to God through the cross, by which he put to death their hostility. He came and preached peace to you who were far away and peace to those who were near. For through him we both have access to the Father by one Spirit.

Consequently, you are no longer foreigners and strangers, but fellow citizens with God's people and also members of his household, built on the foundation of the apostles and prophets, with Christ Jesus himself as the chief cornerstone. In him the whole building is joined together and rises to become a holy temple in the Lord. And in him you too are being built together to become a dwelling in which God lives by his Spirit.

Jesus, a Living Stone

I Peter 2:4-5 gives us a time-honored and much-loved passage about our Lord and how His life is an example to today's Church:

> *"As you come to him, the living Stone—rejected by humans but chosen by God and precious to him—you also, like living stones, are being built into a spiritual house to be a holy priesthood, offering spiritual sacrifices acceptable to God through Jesus Christ."*

A Description of the Church

What should a Church look like? Immediately one thinks of a building, ornate or plain, but with a steeple and possibly a bell. Ask people in town where their Church is, and they will point out a location where a church building sits. Is it any wonder that the modern Church spends so much energy and time in constructing <u>monuments for God</u> rather than <u>ministries for God</u>? A building for the Church can be a useful and effective tool, but it is just that, only a tool … we must think theologically about the Church, not just locally. In fact, if a Church's goal is <u>only</u> to build buildings, it has lost its way.

A Milestone or a Millstone?

Vance Havner, renowned revivalist from the Blue Ridge Mountains of North Carolina, once asked a preacher, "How are you getting along?"

He replied, "We are living in idolatry – just sitting around admiring our new church. We have arrived; we have it made – no more worlds to conquer."

The preacher's irony reveals his insight. His congregation had lost its impetus to further the kingdom of Christ and win the lost for the Lord.

What ought to be a milestone had become a millstone. The modern Church faces the same dilemma. We have run out of goals.

The Church Is People, Not Property

We must be careful in building God's Church … that we see it as <u>people</u> and not <u>property</u>. The Church can survive without buildings or programs, but never without people and God's Spirit. The REAL Church is not built out of <u>concrete blocks</u>, it is built out of <u>consecrated people</u>! The REAL Church cannot be constructed out of *"<u>stumbling blocks</u>"* either, only <u>spiritual blocks</u>!

Jesus Is the Purpose of the Church

The message of the Church must not be compromised. Truth must be spoken at whatever cost, or the Church will lose its *mission* and its *mandate*. We must not lower our standards to become just entertainment or try to just accommodate culture; rather, we must speak to our culture a transformational message that Jesus makes a huge difference. The Church cannot just be another *"feel good"* or *"do good"* organization. It is a *"BE GOOD"* organization, and that is only possible when Christ lives within us.

Becoming a Holy Temple

In Ephesians 2:20, the Bible challenges us as a Church to be a HOLY TEMPLE, that we are *"living stones"* ...

> *"... built upon the foundation of the Apostles and Prophets, with Jesus Christ Himself the chief cornerstone."*

Before we came to know God, we lived as all people do, simply gratifying our sinful and selfish desires. No gathering of unsaved people can possibly be called a *"Church"* just because it is in a building with a sign in front that says so. Before our sins were forgiven, we were *"objects of wrath"* (v. 3b). We could not have been a *"holy temple"* before we knew Christ!

Recycled by God

It is amazing when you think about the material God has used to build a Holy Temple ... He has taken the sinners of this world, people cast aside as useless, and after transforming them by His grace, created the greatest construction project in history, His Church!

Paul's strong language here about how lost we all once were shows the tremendous contrast of God's grace after He changes us. Most builders pick out the finest materials to build a great building, but God has chosen the worst materials to build the greatest building ... He must, however, transform those materials with His Spirit to be useful!

God was the first to use "recycled" materials in a building program!!!

Abiding in God's Truth

When we were away from the real God, our concepts of who and what a "god" is were very different from the reality we now know. As pagans, we were enslaved by our own foolish and darkened hearts! Now, we abide in the light of God's Truth!

What a contrast to being a Christian!

God's Real Holy Temple

We don't build God a temple. He builds us into one! By His grace and love He forgives our sins when we come to Him! There are not enough good works to save anyone. Your works can't be good until you are good, and that only happens after Christ has saved you!

God has taken the sinners of this world and after saving them, brings them together as one in Him! When we belong to Christ, we also belong to one another.

There is only ONE building that is God's Holy Temple! When the temple in Jerusalem was destroyed in 70 A.D., the nation of Israel ceased to exist. It was focused too much on a building and rules ... but God's real temple did not disappear in 70 A.D. It still was there, created out of the many

Christians scattered throughout the Roman Empire, and Rome never could bring this temple down.

Our Importance in Christ

Sometimes we don't appreciate or even realize how important we are together in Christ ... He has made us as believers into a family! After all, the church is called God's house ... and we call God *"Father"* ... and in a house lives a family – the family of God, us! It can be such a wonderful surprise and fill us with joy when we recognize how God has brought us together as His family.

Tammy's Story

I remember reading Tammy Harris' story, that when she turned 21, she began searching for her biological mother. After a year, she had not made much progress. What she didn't know was that her mother, Joyce Schultz, had been trying to locate her for twenty years. According to a recent Associated Press story, there was one more thing Tammy didn't know: Her mother was one of her coworkers at the convenience store where she worked!

One day, Joyce overheard Tammy talking with

another coworker about trying to find her mother. Soon, they were comparing birth certificates. When Tammy realized that the coworker she had known was, in fact, her mother, she fell into her arms.

"We held on for the longest time," Tammy said. "It was the best day of my life."

Each week we rub shoulders with people whom we may barely notice. But if they share a birth in Christ, they are our dearest relatives. How precious is the family of God!

We Have a Job to Do!

Now that we are together as a family in the Church of Jesus Christ, there is a job to do, not just a service we must attend. It is true that we are not saved by our good works, but it is equally true that we are saved to DO good works! (v. 10)

Being the "Church" is a lot more than just physically coming together once a week to sit for a couple of hours ... we have a world to reach with a message of hope and forgiveness.

The Trouble with Tradition

So many times in history, man has tried to build God temples, but so often those temples became more important than God! Worship became a lot of *"dos and don'ts"* more than a vital relationship with a living God.

The approach to God became bogged down with more and more rituals and rules in the buildings, barriers that had to be crossed, more and more doors to go through before you could even hope to come close to God.

This is still the case with many religions today – they make the path to God complicated and long, and so mystical that no one can be sure they have found God!

We must be careful in our churches. Too many times we make it hard for people to come to God … God never made it hard, man did!

Easy Becomes Hard

According to orthodox Jewish tradition, there is only one day between Passover and Pentecost on which anyone may get married or get a haircut.

The grand law of Moses disintegrated into such foolishness that it had to be replaced with the new covenant, written on the hearts of men. This is why Jesus got so angry with the Pharisees. They had made the way to find God so hard that almost no one could do it!

The 10 commandments had become 613

individual statutes *(categorized in two groups, "heavy" and "light")*, and it was nearly impossible for any individual to do them all!

Hard Becomes Easy

Without God, man has no hope. Fortunately, God has made it easy to get to Him. He sent His only Son, Jesus Christ, to die in our place, so that by faith we can be saved.

This is the marvel of the Church, that we are all forgiven sinners! There is real joy in being together now because we are all forgiven!

Our Hope Comes through Jesus

It's been said, "If your religion doesn't take you to church, it is doubtful if it will take you to heaven."

We were without hope outside of Christ! But now in Christ, we who were far off are brought near to God! There is hope for everyone!

Christ died for all. How has God made this change possible? By the blood of Christ through His death for us.

We only have to believe it and preach it, not defend it!

Hungry for God

Henry Ward Beecher, 19th century American Congregationalist clergyman, said that a man who was starving to death would not go into the laboratory to try and figure out how wheat germinates in the soil nor demand a chemical analysis of bread. So those who are really conscious of their need for forgiveness are not concerned with the mechanics of the atonement, but only concerned that they themselves are the recipients of its effects.

People are hungry to know God, although they are not often hungry to be religious! Most people know they are sinners … they just need to know that there is a way to find forgiveness and to know God!

How Simple Is Salvation!

The Gospel is simple enough for a child to come to Christ. We only need to confess we are sinners and ask Christ into our lives.

"By grace" … *"through faith"* … we are saved, *"not of works lest any man should boast"* (vv. 8-9)*!*

Our hope for something better in life comes through Christ. The words of Peter describe the eternal nature and hope of our Lord:

"As you come to him, the living Stone—
rejected by humans but chosen by God and
precious to him—"

1 Peter 2:4

Alive in Christ as Priests unto Him

In Christ we together are a holy temple!

"... you also, like living stones, are being
built into a spiritual house to be a holy
priesthood, offering spiritual sacrifices
acceptable to God through Jesus Christ."

1 Peter 2:5

God's house is alive, not a dead man-made structure!

Attitude Is Better than Architecture!

The world will never be all that impressed with our *buildings* or our *budgets*. What it really needs is to see a vital living Temple that is alive with the love and joy of Christ! In some places, church buildings can look better than the real Church ... how sad! On the other hand, in some places where buildings don't look that great, there can be a vibrant loving temple for God's Spirit to dwell in. We need to make sure the real building or temple of God's Spirit is kept up as well as the facility we so often call the *"Church."* God is more impressed with our ATTITUDE than our ARCHITECTURE. So is the world! So often we can *"look right"* on the outside, but not reflect what we are supposed to stand for. We must be more than *"holy"* in name only!

An Ongoing Building Program

Even now God's temple is continuing to be built. We today rest on the foundation of the Apostles and prophets who have gone before us, on Jesus Christ who is the chief cornerstone.

God has been in a long building program!!! He will not stop building until it is finished! Satan has always tried to destroy God's Temple ... and while he succeeded in bringing down the physical building in Jerusalem in 70 A.D., he will fail with the spiritual Temple, for through Christ, it remains rock solid!

Down through thousands of years, church buildings have been destroyed, governments have taken them away or turned them over for other uses, but never have they destroyed the real *"TEMPLE"* of God, for it is not made from *human goods*, but from the *heart of God*.

Not a Stumbling Block but a Spiritual Block

The *"Holy Temple"* will exist until the end of time. Will you be a part of it? Don't be a *"stumbling block"* ... be a *"spiritual block"* and become part of the greatest building program of all time ... God's Holy Temple! God's Spirit dwells in His Holy Temple ... His Church made up of living stones. Why not get cemented into this structure? Christ will not turn anyone away who comes to Him.

The Jews built a holy temple in Jerusalem for God's dwelling place, but those stones are now mostly gone ... however, God is not gone because His Temple is made from living stones, those who are redeemed by Christ's blood!

God's Spirit lives in His Holy Temple. Are you a part of this great temple? You can be. Let Christ into your life and be a Holy Temple!

The Church Is a Mystery to the World.

This mystery is that through the gospel the Gentiles are heirs together with Israel, members together of one body, and sharers together in the promise in Christ Jesus.

~Paul~

Ephesians
Chapter Three

THE CHURCH

~ *Chapter Three* ~

A MYSTERY

Ephesians 3:1-21

*For this reason I, Paul, the prisoner of
Christ Jesus for the sake of you Gentiles—*

*Surely you have heard about the
administration of God's grace that was
given to me for you, that is, the mystery
made known to me by revelation, as I have
already written briefly. In reading this,
then, you will be able to understand my
insight into the mystery of Christ, which
was not made known to people in other*

generations as it has now been revealed by the Spirit to God's holy apostles and prophets. This mystery is that through the gospel the Gentiles are heirs together with Israel, members together of one body, and sharers together in the promise in Christ Jesus.

I became a servant of this gospel by the gift of God's grace given me through the working of his power. Although I am less than the least of all the Lord's people, this grace was given me: to preach to the Gentiles the boundless riches of Christ, and to make plain to everyone the administration of this mystery, which for ages past was kept hidden in God, who created all things. His intent was that now, through the church, the manifold wisdom of God should be made known to the rulers and authorities in the heavenly realms, according to his eternal purpose that he accomplished in Christ Jesus our Lord. In him and through faith in him we may approach God with freedom and confidence. I ask you, therefore, not to be discouraged because of my sufferings for you, which are your glory.

*For this reason I kneel before the Father,
from whom every family in heaven and on
earth derives its name. I pray that out of
his glorious riches he may strengthen you
with power through his Spirit in your inner
being, so that Christ may dwell in your
hearts through faith. And I pray that you,
being rooted and established in love, may
have power, together with all the Lord's
holy people, to grasp how wide and long
and high and deep is the love of Christ,
and to know this love that surpasses
knowledge—that you may be filled to the
measure of all the fullness of God.*

*Now to him who is able to do
immeasurably more than all we ask or
imagine, according to his power that is at
work within us, to him be glory in the
church and in Christ Jesus throughout all
generations, for ever and ever! Amen.*

Positive Wonder and Negative Scorn

Why is it the Church gets so much attention in
this world, both good and bad? It is often the focus
of this world's positive wonder and negative

scorn. Why? Along with politics, religion stirs up more debate, attention, and intrigue than any other subject.

Both a Mystery and a Love Story

Somebody has said that there are two kinds of books that always sell well: mysteries and love stories. The Gospel is both. It is a mystery, long hidden, at last revealed. It is a love story in the finest sense of that word. It unveils God's love for the world and for us.

The world has never been able to explain the continued power and presence of the Church around the world. So many other organizations that have faced hostile political pressures have simply disappeared, businesses that have experienced poor economic times have folded up their tents and vanished from the landscape of this world, groups that have been attacked and persecuted have surrendered. BUT, the Church has withstood all these troubling circumstances and much more and is stronger and larger today than ever before! How, and why? This really is a mystery – but one whose secret is revealed in the Bible!

Supernatural Power!

The continued success and existence of the Church through 2,000 years of turmoil and trouble can only be explained by one thing ... *God's supernatural power!*

> *"... 'Not by might nor by power, but by my Spirit,' says the LORD Almighty."*

Zechariah 4:6

"Might" – could mean political or financial power; *"power"* – could mean human effort. It is ONLY by His Spirit that the Church marches on!

God's Enemy Becomes God's Champion

Paul was hardly the choice for a Christian, much less an Apostle! He once literally murdered people who called themselves Christians! He hated the Church prior to his conversion experience. He wasn't much to look at, was cocky, and he was sure he was right about everything before Christ confronted him.

He was hardly the kind of person we usually associate with love and peace!

God's love and grace alone is a mystery. Why He bestowed it on people like Saul of Tarsus, or characters like you and me is itself a mystery!

Grace Replaces Rituals

The "way" to God used to be complicated and difficult ... now by God's sacrifice and grace it is so easy. Gone is much of the mystery! While religion can make it hard to come to God, Jesus' blood has opened the way freely for all to come.

The mystery about God's grace wasn't clear until Christ came and died. The way to God before Jesus came had been full of rituals and complicated processes, but in Christ the door is wide open and even the most unworthy of people can march into God's presence through the redemptive blood of Christ!

God's grace was intended to do one thing no political or economic power has ever been able to ... unite the most disparate of people into one body, His Church! Christ does it by changing the person from the inside out; the world tries to unite people by changing things from the outside in. Christ's offer of *"freedom from sin"* unites us, the mystery of God's grace at work in the hearts and lives of sinners! If political freedom can move so many, just think what spiritual freedom can do!

Freedom in Holy Righteousness

Some nations offer freedom in the form of human rights, but Christ offers freedom in the form of holy righteousness! Christ brought together Jews and Gentiles in Paul's day … in his day they often hated each other! Christ brings together black and white, rich and poor, educated and uneducated, powerful and weak, and makes them one in Him! What other power on earth can do this?

Yes, the Church is a mystery. It makes no sense to the outsider. They can't see what unites us, that it is Jesus Christ and His Spirit! But it must not be a mystery to us! We must always remember what unites us! It isn't our great ideas, our programs, our philosophy or styles; it is the power of God's Spirit that makes us one!

Changed from Sinner to Saint

So, what does the Spirit use to draw us? The *"gospel"* … the *"good news"* of salvation!

Preaching the Gospel is hardly the kind of device the world would use to transform human beings into a loving body of believers! Yet, this is precisely how the Spirit energizes people, turning them from sinner to saint … and the world doesn't get it!

Paul stated this amazing truth in 1 Corinthians 1:18:

"For the message of the cross is foolishness to those who are perishing, but to us who are being saved it is the power of God."

He goes on in 1 Corinthians 2:14:

"The man without the Spirit does not accept the things that come from the Spirit of God, for they are foolishness to him, and he cannot understand them, because they are spiritually discerned."

Preaching the Gospel has power, the power of God's Spirit, so it not only transforms the lives of those that hear it and respond, but it also transforms those who tell it!

The Power in Preaching the Gospel

The world has never figured out the power of preaching the Gospel ... nothing on earth has so transformed the world as Christ's death and resurrection! It is the power of God's Spirit in preaching that moves people's hearts. The message is from

God and not man, and that is the primary difference! It is no mystery that God's Word should have God's power in it, for the Spirit is the author of the Word!

God is making His presence and power known through His Church! It is critical that a Church be what it should be ... God's reputation could hang on our reputation! It is through the Church that God makes known His manifest wisdom! When we say we are Christians the world expects certain things ... they expect the best of what God has, not the worst. It is important we live up to His name!

A Man Named Cassius

The boxer we know as Muhammad Ali began his life as Cassius Clay. He changed his name, saying that Clay was a name that came from slavery and he would not wear it any longer.

What he did not know was this: the Cassius Clay for whom he was named was a fiery opponent of slavery. He opposed it at a time when it was quite dangerous to do so. On the other hand, the original Muhammad Ali did nothing to replace slavery with freedom.

As Christians we wear the name of the one who set us free.

Sons and Daughters of the Most High

The world can't imagine the power of the name *"Christian,"* meaning *"Christ-like"* … in fact, it is often scoffed at. But there is a reality to that name that defies the world. In that name, Christ is unveiled and His love and forgiveness are made known to us and to others.

No matter the world's attitude toward that name, it is the mystery of God's love unveiled in a dark world … the Church marches on as Christ's standard bearers! The only way we can receive entrance into Christ's Church is through humble recognition that we are a sinner. No well-known name, no power of family lineage, no office can bring us into favor with God, only our humble recognition that we are sinners in need of His grace … and then He changes everything and makes us sons and daughters of the most High God!!

We dare not come any other way; no braggadocio foolishness will gain us entrance to God's salvation, only brokenness and faith.

Standing on Equal Ground

We stand on equal ground when we come to Christ – as sinners – and we stand on equal ground when Christ has saved us – as saints, brothers and sisters in Christ! The Gospel reveals that this has been Christ's plan all along, to perform His work in the world through His Church energized by His Spirit ... not through the political, economic and educational aspects of this world. We must never forget this in building His Church! Use everything else as tools to reach the world but rely on the Spirit for power to save the lost!

The Gates of Hell Shall Not Prevail

Another "mystery" about the Church is its survival these past two millennia! Again, this only proves the reality of the Spirit's power behind the Church. What other institution or nation has lasted this long? The Church's success is not contingent on man's power; it is based on God's power, and thus *unshakable!* Too many times Christians fret over the surrounding evil and act as though the Church could go under any moment. We must remember that nothing on earth is more unshakable than the Church!!! Jesus said the *"gates of Hell shall not destroy her"* (Matt. 16:18). We must guard our focus and faith in this world.

Blanketed by God's Love

Many times, we have heard it said that the

Church is surrounded by an evil and hostile world, like a besieged fortress. We need to remember that it is also true that the Church is surrounded by God's love and care! Individually and collectively, we are blanketed by God's love as the earth is blanketed by the atmosphere. God loves the Church and will never forsake her.

We have an unshakable message from an unshakable God, and so, as the unshakable Church, why are we afraid to speak out? We are *"rooted"* in Christ! We have God's Spirit to empower the message and the messenger ... this is Paul's point in Ephesians 3:17b-19:

> *"... And I pray that you, being rooted and established in love, may have power, together with all the saints, to grasp how wide and long and high and deep is the love of Christ, and to know this love that surpasses knowledge—that you may be filled to the measure of all the fullness of God."*

Let the Church move and let it be bold!

It Is the Day of Satan's Defeat

God WILL do more than we can imagine or

think ... or ask! We are the ones that so often limit God. He can with one stroke accomplish things that no man can do!

Our sword is the sword of the Spirit as described in the Bible, and it can cut loose any knot that would bind people up! If Christ could defeat Satan 2,000 years ago and rise triumphantly over the tomb, then He can handle anything that is coming in this age, and so can His Church when it is dependent on His Spirit for power! We cannot fail, because Christ cannot fail!

We act on what we believe, so our actions reflect the level of belief we truly have! If we don't believe in God, things don't happen ... He is ready to do *"IMMEASURABLY MORE THAN WE ASK OR IMAGINE ..."*

It is tragic when we don't act on this! The Church need NOT be weak and ineffective in this world; God's Spirit is ready to work through people of faith! We underestimate God, and so does the world!

What Does God Expect of You?

Now the real questions! Now that you understand some of the mystery and the marvel of God's desire to empower His saints and His Church ... what is it that God wants you to do? Don't limit

Him, trust Him! Develop a plan of action consistent with His character and calling. Follow through … and watch the mystery of godliness worked out!

The Church's Power Revealed!

The Church is a true mystery! How has it existed through so many political contexts, from persecution to prosperity? The only explanation for the Church's continued success and existence is the power of the Gospel – the good news that anyone can know God's love and peace. In the natural, the Church would be doomed to failure, but because it is invested with power that is supernatural, it cannot be a failure! The Church's power comes from the Gospel and God's people living together in Christ's love.

The Church Is a New Man in Christ.

Instead, speaking the truth in love, we will grow to become in every respect the mature body of him who is the head, that is, Christ.

~Paul~

Ephesians
Chapter Four

THE CHURCH

~ Chapter Four ~

A NEW MAN

Ephesians 4:1-32

As a prisoner for the Lord, then, I urge you to live a life worthy of the calling you have received. Be completely humble and gentle; be patient, bearing with one another in love. Make every effort to keep the unity of the Spirit through the bond of peace. There is one body and one Spirit, just as you were called to one hope when you were called; one Lord, one faith, one baptism; one God and Father of all, who is over all and through all and in all.

But to each one of us grace has been given as Christ apportioned it. This is why it says:

"When he ascended on high, he took many captives and gave gifts to his people."

(What does "he ascended" mean except that he also descended to the lower, earthly regions? He who descended is the very one who ascended higher than all the heavens, in order to fill the whole universe.) So Christ himself gave the apostles, the prophets, the evangelists, the pastors and teachers, to equip his people for works of service, so that the body of Christ may be built up until we all reach unity in the faith and in the knowledge of the Son of God and become mature, attaining to the whole measure of the fullness of Christ.

Then we will no longer be infants, tossed back and forth by the waves, and blown here and there by every wind of teaching and by the cunning and craftiness of people in their deceitful scheming. Instead,

*speaking the truth in love, we will grow to
become in every respect the mature body
of him who is the head, that is, Christ.
From him the whole body, joined and held
together by every supporting ligament,
grows and builds itself up in love, as each
part does its work.*

*So I tell you this, and insist on it in the
Lord, that you must no longer live as the
Gentiles do, in the futility of their thinking.
They are darkened in their understanding
and separated from the life of God because
of the ignorance that is in them due to the
hardening of their hearts. Having lost all
sensitivity, they have given themselves
over to sensuality so as to indulge in every
kind of impurity, and they are full of greed.*

*That, however, is not the way of life you
learned when you heard about Christ and
were taught in him in accordance with the
truth that is in Jesus. You were taught,
with regard to your former way of life, to
put off your old self, which is being
corrupted by its deceitful desires; to be
made new in the attitude of your minds;
and to put on the new self, created to be*

like God in true righteousness and holiness.

Therefore each of you must put off falsehood and speak truthfully to your neighbor, for we are all members of one body. "In your anger do not sin": Do not let the sun go down while you are still angry, and do not give the devil a foothold. Anyone who has been stealing must steal no longer, but must work, doing something useful with their own hands, that they may have something to share with those in need.

Do not let any unwholesome talk come out of your mouths, but only what is helpful for building others up according to their needs, that it may benefit those who listen. And do not grieve the Holy Spirit of God, with whom you were sealed for the day of redemption. Get rid of all bitterness, rage and anger, brawling and slander, along with every form of malice. Be kind and compassionate to one another, forgiving each other, just as in Christ God forgave you.

A Time of Easy Credit

We are living at a time when one can join just about anything without having to change anything or make any serious commitments. My email program is flooded daily with requests to join everything under the sun. The qualifications are usually stated something like this:

"Nothing Down"

"No Minimum Purchase Required"

"YOU CAN'T BE TURNED DOWN"

"No Payments Until Next Year"

"You Don't Have to Do Anything Now"

In other words, all you have to do to qualify is be living and breathing ... oh and have money! Let me assure you that in God's kingdom IT IS DIF-FERENT. Big changes are expected and required! While it only requires faith and confession to find a new life in Christ, it requires a changed per-spective and behavior once we have come to Christ. We must *"put off the old self"* (v. 22) and then *"put on the new"* (v. 23).

The biggest hindrance for unbelievers accept-ing authentic Christianity is often not doctrinal or theological, it is the lack of finding truly transformed believers whose lives give witness to the power of change the Holy Spirit makes in us. The name *"Christian"* should match the reality!

A Street that Doesn't Live Up to Its Name

In one Polish city there is a street named Beautiful. It is probably the ugliest street in town. Unpaved, it is filled with ruts and potholes, and to drive faster than five miles an hour would be unthinkable. Obviously, the street didn't turn out the way planners had hoped. Being "NEW" is not an option when we come to Christ … everything changes, all things become new … and it must show to the world, to the Church, and to our family and friends!

We Are a NEW CREATION!

The Bible teaches us that in Christ we become a *"NEW CREATION."* This means the Church is a *"NEW CREATION"* also. There is nothing in this world like the Church or the Christian … and the world must see revolutionary lives, lives transformed by God's power.

Ultimately, it is not so much our *beliefs* that teach the world about Christianity as much as it is our *behavior!* (This mirrors Paul's comments about us being *"letters read by everybody"* in 2 Cor. 3:2.) Paul is quite clear about his passion for living correctly before God and this world … he says, *"I urge you …"* It is no mere suggestion; Paul's point is simple: *"If you belong to Christ, your behavior does too!"*

We are called to live a life *"worthy of the calling"* we have received in Christ. Too often people who claim to be believers talk as if God is real but act as if He is not. Humility, gentleness, patience, bearing with one another in love, peace and unity are the norm for Christian living, not the exception. No matter our position, we need to be sensitive to one another, to reflect the very character of Christ … to even be careful about using truth to hurt one another!

We Are Responsible for KEEPING THE PEACE!

Notice that while God is the one that grants peace and unity, we are the ones responsible for *"keeping it."* Ephesians 4:3 says that we are to:

"Make every effort to keep the unity of the Spirit through the bond of peace."

We have responsibilities for fleshing out God's graces! It is not an automatic thing or forced on us by God. We must be passionate about God's graces, not just in *principle* but also in *practice!!*

We Are to Be a COMMITTED FAMILY!

Paul now strongly develops the theme of *"oneness"* for the Church! Diversity in unity! The Church cannot afford to divide itself. At stake is the witness of the Gospel which has the power to make us into one body, His Church! Unity cannot be achieved by casualness in commitments; the Church cannot afford *"casual relationships"* characterized by a lack of commitment. It is not enough to simply park yourself in a Church body; you must participate in its life and commitments! The Church doesn't need *"hitchhikers"* … it needs *"family"* members!

No One Is Greater than Another

In the Church, *"one is not the loneliest number"* … it is the number of God's unity and power! We are to be joined as one with the other believers around us.

So great is the call to be united that it is mandated above personal rights! It is more important to be right with each other than simply to be right on an issue. Mutual relationship is greater than personal rights! This was demonstrated by Christ Himself on the cross ... He died though He had done nothing wrong. Because He wanted a relationship with us, He willingly gave up His rights to reunite us to God.

In a culture that has elevated *"my rights"* above everything else, this will be a challenge for the believer, but it is still a must! We are different from this world! We are new creatures; we must die to the old ways. God puts a premium on unity, so should we.

Diversity Unites the Church

Unity doesn't mean we all do the same thing, just that we love the same way. God gifts us differently in His body so we can minister to one another and to the world.

This diversity, however, is not meant to divide us, but to unite us. No one should elevate himself or herself above anyone else; we are in this together for mutual benefit and growth. The Church will never accomplish the tasks of ministry if we don't work together in unity!

There is no power in disunity, especially in God's Church!

Disunity Never Triumphs

I remember hearing a story used in a sermon illustration ... a man went to an asylum for the criminally insane. He was a bit surprised to find that there were three guards to take care of a hundred inmates.

He said to one of the guards, "Aren't you afraid that the inmates will unite, overcome you, and escape?"

The guard replied, "Lunatics never unite."

How true! Think of one of the smallest creatures on the earth, the locust. Individually, they have no power at all. They can be easily crushed and cast aside. Yet, when they unite into swarms of millions, they decimate the landscape.

We must unite to be strong. Locusts do. Christians should. If we don't, we will never release the power God has in store for us.

You Have a Gift in the Church

What are you doing to contribute to the unity of the Church, or to its disunity? Each gift is given with the purpose of building up the whole. The Church cannot afford to neglect any gift given by God. The purpose of these gifts in an atmosphere of unity *"is to prepare God's people for works of service"* (v. 12). You will note that all of God's gifts are given to *"BUILD UP"* His Church, not tear it down! So called "gifts" that tear down a Church are not God's gifts! The fruit of unity with gifts is not only works of service, but maturity of the saints!

God's Gifts Produce Maturity

The function of God's gifts in an atmosphere of loving unity produces maturity. Such maturity brings stability. Such a Church will be protected against schemes and attempts to confuse. This kind of environment broadens the horizons of the believer; he or she doesn't grow up with a narrow understanding of God's plan for unity. "Individualism" makes one small! We cannot grow much by ourselves. We are too small alone! Disconnected believers from a Church body never develop the potential God has for them. This *"new self"* can only grow well when it is united to a body.

To Be in Christ Means to Be Changed!

Paul's language here again tells us how important the issue of "being different" or "new" is once we are in Christ!

"So I tell you this, and insist on it in the Lord, that you must no longer live as the Gentiles do ..."

Ephesians 4:17

We MUST not live as we did before we received Christ ... we MUST live differently or we make a mockery out of God's grace. We cheapen it! If we have been delivered out of this world, let us show it!

A Lesson from Charles Spurgeon

Charles Spurgeon, an influential 19th century Baptist preacher, tells this story:

One of the ancient fathers, we are told, had lived with a woman before his conversion, and a short time after she accosted him as usual. Knowing how likely he was to fall into sin, he ran away with all his might, and she ran after him, crying, "Why do you run away? It's only me."

He answered, "I run away because I am not myself. I am a new man."

Let us not be ashamed of being "new" or different than we once were. We should be better and not worse! The witness of the Gospel is often judged by the reality of change in our lives!

We Must Avoid Returning to the Ways of the World

The unbelievers of this world live in the fantasy of things being just fine, yet their understanding is darkened by sin and they can't even see their lostness unless the light of the Gospel shines in on their hearts and conscience!

We must not be like that now that we have found Christ. In Christ we have been healed and can fly again. We must be careful to avoid returning to the empty ways of this world.

Paul reminds us that outside of Christ we live to satisfy whatever whim comes into our hearts ... this often leads to painful consequences in sin. We don't have to live that way anymore; in fact, we MUST not live that way anymore! We are to live in a way to avoid the pitfalls of this world.

The Proof of the Gospel IN US!

The world needs *"proof"* of the power of the Gospel! Where will they find it? IN US! But only if we *"put off the old self and put on the new."* What this world needs are more examples of godly people, not more arguments about God's existence!

We may not all be well versed in science to stand toe to toe in a debate, but we can stand tall as examples of God's grace ... there is no argument against a godly example!!! The world won't be changed by TEXTBOOK LECTURES as much as it will by TRANSFORMED LIVES!

We Must DEMONSTRATE Our New Self

Paul's final remarks in this section deal with demonstrating the putting off of our *"OLD SELF"* (vv. 26-31).
1. Don't sin with the wrong use of anger!
2. Those who once stole must stop stealing and work and earn a living!
3. Don't let unwholesome talk come out of our mouths but build one another up.
4. Don't grieve the Holy Spirit.
5. Cooperate with God's Spirit.
6. Get rid of ALL bitterness, rage, anger, brawling, slander, and malice.

The Positive Side of Putting On Our New Self!

Paul ends this section by adding the positive

behaviors that come when we put on the *"NEW SELF"* (v. 32).

1. We are to show kindness to one another.

2. We are to forgive one another.

There is great power in forgiveness, for it is the very example of God's love for us ... and when we put on the *"NEW SELF"* it means putting on the same garment of *"forgiveness"* toward others! Forgiveness reveals the power of God, and it is a need down deep in the heart of every human being!

A Father and His Son

Ernest Hemingway wrote a story about a father and his teenage son. In the story, the relationship had become somewhat strained, and the teenage son ran away from home. His father began a journey in search of that rebellious son. Finally, in Madrid, Spain, in a last, desperate attempt to find the boy, the father put an ad in the local newspaper.

The ad read: "Dear Paco, Meet me in front of the newspaper office at noon. All is forgiven. I love you. Your father."

The next day, in front of the newspaper office, eight hundred Pacos showed up. They were all seeking forgiveness. They were all seeking the love of their father.

Our Proof to the World

We really show proof to the world that the Gospel has power when we forgive, for this shows the *"NEW SELF"* we have in Christ! The Church, like the Christian, is a *"NEW MAN"* ... the old has died and a new has emerged. But we must give the new life expression.

The other side of this is that we must avoid returning to the old. Do others know that you are different since you found Christ? Is the old self dead and the new self demonstrating proof of God's power?

Confession Brings Conversion!

The first step in salvation is confession of sins and of Christ as Lord – but this is only the INITIAL step. After this first step comes conversion! Conversion means becoming something NEW – it is a process of becoming what we are in Christ, a NEW MAN or NEW WOMAN! It means "change" – from the old ways to the new ways, God's ways! How's the development of the "NEW" going in your life – is the change apparent to God, to you, to others? It MUST be! We are a new creation in Christ, so let the world see it!

The Church Is the Bride of Christ.

*For you were once darkness, but now you
are light in the Lord. Live as children of
light (for the fruit of the light consists in
all goodness, righteousness and truth) and
find out what pleases the Lord.*

~Paul~

Ephesians
Chapter Five

~ Chapter Five ~

A BRIDE

Ephesians 5:1-33

*Follow God's example, therefore, as
dearly loved children and walk in the way
of love, just as Christ loved us and gave
himself up for us as a fragrant offering
and sacrifice to God.*

*But among you there must not be even a
hint of sexual immorality, or of any kind of
impurity, or of greed, because these are
improper for God's holy people. Nor
should there be obscenity, foolish talk or*

coarse joking, which are out of place, but rather thanksgiving. For of this you can be sure: No immoral, impure or greedy person—such a person is an idolater—has any inheritance in the kingdom of Christ and of God. Let no one deceive you with empty words, for because of such things God's wrath comes on those who are disobedient. Therefore do not be partners with them.

For you were once darkness, but now you are light in the Lord. Live as children of light (for the fruit of the light consists in all goodness, righteousness and truth) and find out what pleases the Lord. Have nothing to do with the fruitless deeds of darkness, but rather expose them. It is shameful even to mention what the disobedient do in secret. But everything exposed by the light becomes visible—and everything that is illuminated becomes a light. This is why it is said:

"Wake up, sleeper, rise from the dead, and Christ will shine on you."

Be very careful, then, how you live—not as

unwise but as wise, making the most of every opportunity, because the days are evil. Therefore do not be foolish but understand what the Lord's will is. Do not get drunk on wine, which leads to debauchery. Instead, be filled with the Spirit, speaking to one another with psalms, hymns, and songs from the Spirit. Sing and make music from your heart to the Lord, always giving thanks to God the Father for everything, in the name of our Lord Jesus Christ.

Submit to one another out of reverence for Christ.

Wives, submit yourselves to your own husbands as you do to the Lord. For the husband is the head of the wife as Christ is the head of the church, his body, of which he is the Savior. Now as the church submits to Christ, so also wives should submit to their husbands in everything.

Husbands, love your wives, just as Christ loved the church and gave himself up for her to make her holy, cleansing her by the washing with water through the word, and to present her to himself as a radiant church, without stain or wrinkle or any other blemish, but holy and blameless. In this same way, husbands ought to love their wives as their own bodies. He who loves his wife loves himself. After all, no one ever hated their own body, but they feed and care for their body, just as Christ does the church—for we are members of his body. "For this reason a man will leave his father and mother and be united to his wife, and the two will become one flesh." This is a profound mystery—but I am talking about Christ and the church. However, each one of you also must love his wife as he loves himself, and the wife must respect her husband.

A Fundamental Relationship

No relationship on earth is more fundamental than the marriage relationship. Ultimately, the very core of our culture and civilization rests on this basic institution. This is also why the religious and non-religious alike become alarmed when the marriage relationship breaks down or is in trouble.

Marriage is the most intimate of all relationships on earth, even above parent and child! When God wanted to express the love He has for His people, He could not have chosen a more powerful image than to liken the Church to being His bride.

A bride and groom are passionately in love; they can think of nothing else but each other. It is an obsession! Such is the love God has for His Church, His bride ... and what He desires us to have for Him. When we love like this, our every thought and expression find their way to God and are about God.

A Covenantal Relationship

The Bible teaches us that the Church is like a bride and that God desires a covenantal relationship with each believer. The Church is much more than an institution, and like marriage, the relationships are sacred to God.

Before Paul discusses the marriage relationship, he discusses the individual's responsibilities before God. One cannot have a good marriage if the individuals are not good! It is critical to evaluate the other person before entering into marriage. Christ wants His bride to live a pure life.

The Responsibilities God Places on Us

Paul outlines the responsibilities of the individual as a part of the bride of Christ. Paul begins the positive aspects first:

"Imitators of God"
   "Live a life of love"
      "Sacrificial living"

Paul uses Christ as our example. If we base our behaviors on the life modeled by our Lord, we will be the pure bride God desires to see in us.

Behaviors to Avoid

Negative issues that will create an undesirable relationship with our Lord:

"Obscenity"
"Foolish talk or coarse joking"
"Immorality"
"Impurity"
"Greed"
"Idolatry"

God desires us to live "above" the standards of this world.

Living a Worthy Life

We came out of such darkness, and as the bride of Christ we are to demonstrate a life worthy of Christ's love and cleansing. God wants a pure bride. Once we have been delivered from such sin, we must not return to it again. When we seek to marry someone, we want to know that their heart is fully devoted to us, and that their previous corrupt lifestyle is over and they are ready to settle down in a committed and loving relationship.

Purity Isn't by Chance!

A pure lifestyle doesn't happen by accident! Paul tells individual believers to continually prepare themselves to live holy. Paul says, *"Be very careful, then, how you live—not as unwise but as wise"* (v. 15). One cannot live a godly life by accident or without planning to. We must not be casual about sin in our own lives. It is critical to be careful.

In biblical days there were those who were sloppy about their commitment, and they crashed their faith and relationship with God. So can we. King Saul in the Old Testament threw away his relationship with God. Judas was careless and paid a heavy price. Demas had served God but then got careless … notice Paul's positive comment about Demas in his letter to the Colossians:

"Our dear friend Luke, the doctor, and Demas send greetings."

Colossians 4:14

… but later he says to Timothy:

"… for Demas, because he loved this world, has deserted me and has gone to Thessalonica."

2 Timothy 4:10

We must not let our guard down!

A Lesson from Hollywood

In the movie *Casualties of War*, Michael J. Fox plays Private Erikson, a soldier in Vietnam who is part of a squad that abducts and rapes a young Vietnamese girl. He didn't participate in the crime. Afterward, as he struggles with what has happened, he says to the other men in his squad, *"Just because each of us might at any second be blown away, we're acting like we can do anything we want, as though it doesn't matter what we do. I'm thinking it's just the opposite. Because we might be dead in the next split-second, maybe we got to be extra careful what we do. Because maybe it matters more. Maybe it matters more than we ever know."*

Death, for all of us, is a breath away. And the nearer death is, the closer we are to answering to God for all we have said and done.

Our Chance to Excel!

We must be uncompromising with sin, especially as the bride of Christ! Before Paul addresses the marriage relationship, he addresses who they are as individuals. We don't primarily change after we are married from what we were before marriage, at least not without great effort. Paul challenges us to be better than we were alone.

Paul returns to the positive at the end of his list:

"... making the most of every opportunity, ..."
"... understand what the Lord's will is."
"... be filled with the Spirit."
"Speak to one another with psalms, hymns and spiritual songs. Sing and make music in your heart to the Lord."
"... always giving thanks ..."

A Relational Comparison to Christ

Paul now addresses human marriage as a symbol of the relationship of Christ with His Church. He begins by stating that they should mutually submit to each other. This speaks of respect and love, not lording over one member, but caring for each other equally. It is vital not to leave out the first verse in this passage when covering these verses.

"Submit to one another out of reverence for Christ."

Ephesians 5:21

Some men like to quote the next verse only. In doing so, they mislead and misconstrue the meaning of this passage and create division in their relationships.

"Wives, submit to your husbands as to the Lord."

Ephesians 5:22

Our Submission Is a CHOICE!

The idea of *"submit"* here is often misunderstood. FIRST, it is in the MIDDLE VOICE in Greek, meaning a voluntary desire or attitude to contribute, not by force or decree, but by volition. This is an act of love, submitting on the inside and not just the outside. It indicates a sense of safety and peace based on the loving character of the husband. It is not a call for wives to be forced to submit.

There are three verses written to the woman and nine to the man ... where do you think the greater problem was? The three verses cannot be stripped away from the command of Paul to husbands, which is for them to love their wife like Christ loved the Church! A wife will find it a joy to submit to a man who loves her, sacrifices for her, and is willing to lay down his own life for her! Try praising your wife even if it does frighten her at first. A husband won't have problems loving a wife who cares for his best interests either!

Freedom to Love

Love seeks to free, not control. Christ loves His Church, sets us free from sin's dominion, and we become free to love Him back with a heart that desires to submit to Him. Husbands, your wife is your partner, not your enemy or servant! Wives, your husband is your partner, not your enemy! It is an amazing relationship, and powerful! Such is the Church also! Love levels the playing field!

Marriage Is Permanent

Marriage was meant by God to be a permanent relationship of husband and wife. We leave our parents, but not our spouses! We build our lives together, working together, loving together, and growing together in marriage. This is the idea of *"become one flesh"* (Mark 10:8) ... a joining that is complete. While Paul relates his comments here to a man and woman, he also states that what he says also applies to the *"mystery"* that is the Church, the bride of Christ. There is strength in being united ... a power to live in a way beyond the strength of a single person.

We Are Stronger When We Are United

The Church is triumphant when united to Christ ... not even Hell can prevail against the bride of Christ! The mutual love and sacrifice will create a bond so powerful that all the demons in Hell cannot fight it! Our earthly marriages should reflect the image of the heavenly one. When we realize the power of the sacrifice Christ has made for His Church, we cannot fail to fall in love with our Lord! He chose to die to be with us!

The Bond of Love

In *Man in the Mirror*, Patrick Morley tells of a group of fishermen who landed in a secluded bay in Alaska and had a great day fishing for salmon. But when they returned to their sea plane, they found it aground because of the fluctuating tides. They waited until the next morning for the tide to come in, but when they took off, they only got a few feet into the air before crashing back into the sea.

Being aground the day before had punctured one of the pontoons, and it had filled up with water. The sea plane slowly began to sink. The passengers, three men and a 12-year-old son of one of the men, prayed and then jumped into the icy cold waters to swim to shore.

The riptide was strong, but two of the men reached the shore exhausted. They looked back and saw the father with his arms around his son being swept out to sea. The boy had not been strong enough to make it. The father was a strong swimmer, but he had chosen to die with his son rather than to live without him.

An Irresistible Love!

The power of this kind of love is irresistible! Both as the bride of Christ and as examples of marriage, we are to live in such a way as to demonstrate the power of God's love and commitment to us. Jesus one day will return for His bride! Will you be ready to join Him forever in eternity?

We Are the Bride of Christ

The Church is the bride of Christ. As such, Christ died for her, He has nurtured her, and He has put the needs of the Church above His own.

Christ loves His Church passionately and desires the Church to live a pure life, thus giving testimony to the exalted position she has in this world.

This relationship of Christ and His bride is a permanent one, the image of marriage presented from the beginning of time. The importance of this picture of the Church as the bride of Christ speaks about relationships; we are not just an institution but the very bride of Christ.

The Church Is a Soldier of Christ.

Finally, be strong in the Lord and in his mighty power. Put on the full armor of God, so that you can take your stand against the devil's schemes.

~Paul~

Ephesians
Chapter Six

~ *Chapter Six* ~

A SOLDIER

Ephesians 6:10-24

Finally, be strong in the Lord and in his mighty power. Put on the full armor of God, so that you can take your stand against the devil's schemes. For our struggle is not against flesh and blood, but against the rulers, against the authorities, against the powers of this dark world and against the spiritual forces of evil in the heavenly realms. Therefore put on the full armor of God, so that when the day of evil comes, you may be able to stand your ground, and after you have done everything, to stand. Stand firm then, with the belt of truth buckled around your waist, with the breastplate of righteousness in place, and with your feet fitted with the readiness that comes from the gospel of peace. In addition to all this, take up the shield of faith, with which you can extinguish all the flaming arrows of the evil one. Take the helmet of salvation and the sword of the Spirit, which is the word of God.

And pray in the Spirit on all occasions with all kinds of prayers and requests. With this in mind, be alert and always keep on praying for all the Lord's people. Pray also for me, that whenever I speak, words may be given me so that I will fearlessly make known the mystery of the gospel, for which I am an ambassador in chains. Pray that I may declare it fearlessly, as I should.

Tychicus, the dear brother and faithful servant in the Lord, will tell you everything, so that you also may know how I am and what I am doing. I am sending him to you for this very purpose, that you may know how we are, and that he may encourage you.

Peace to the brothers and sisters, and love with faith from God the Father and the Lord Jesus Christ. Grace to all who love our Lord Jesus Christ with an undying love.

Equipped for Battle

The quality of soldiers and the quality of equipment they use often determine the difference between an army winning a war and losing one. Could you imagine the United States of America sending into battle the weak and sickly with clubs and sticks to fight a modern, well-equipped enemy army!!? Yet how many times does the Church fight with their weakest warriors and without proper equipment? The war against sin is a winnable war; the fight against Satan and his minions is doable and will end in victory IF we properly equip ourselves for battle.

Becoming a Christian and living successfully as one is a battle! We live in days when the forces of evil are growing around the world. Satan knows his end is coming sooner than ever, and his efforts at lashing out against God and His people will only intensify!

The Christian Soldier

Paul explains that the Church is like a soldier. Arrayed for battle and properly equipped, she will be victorious. But we need to take seriously the nature of the battle that we are in. It is a serious battle, and the Church must be engaged in warfare as a well-equipped soldier!

A Very Real War

We live on a battlefield facing a very real enemy. This warfare is real, and so is the equipment we need to successfully engage the enemy to win. The war is winnable, however, and we will triumph in the end! Paul was not writing from a cruise ship, but from prison! You would think Paul was powerless ... each day a new soldier arrived and chained himself to the Apostle Paul. Interestingly enough, the armor Paul mentions is in the exact order a Roman soldier put each piece on.

Paul was only a prisoner by chains, but he was free spiritually! Paul's power was greater than the soldier he was chained to, and the battle he was engaged in was more important than the battles the Roman soldier would fight.

The greatest battles require the greatest courage and faith ... Paul was not afraid. Are you afraid to stand up and fight for God? The greater challenge will require greater courage but will also mean greater victory!

History Teaches Us a Lesson

When Napoleon was an artillery officer at the siege of Toulon, he built a battery in such an exposed position that he was told he would never find men to man it. But Napoleon had a sure instinct for what was required. He put up a sign saying The Battery of Men without Fear, and the battery was always manned.

Our Strength Is Not Our Own

You will note that Paul does NOT say, *"Be strong WITH the Lord ..."* but *"Be strong IN the Lord ..."* Our power comes from being IN Christ, and not just our natural abilities. We fight with God's power and not our own.

We will *"struggle"* ... but not against flesh and blood! There are real evil powers in this world ...

and unless someone is completely blind, they can see and hear about it every day on the news!

To fight without God's strength is a losing battle. Unless one has the conviction of greater strength and power and of support, he will collapse under the weight! It would be a losing battle against such forces if we didn't realize that Christ is fighting with us and for us!

Support is critical for soldiers ... they need the morale and encouragement of their fellow soldiers also!

Wearing the Proper Armor

The powers we struggle against are real, but they can be defeated if we go in God's strength and with His equipment ... and we fight together! Let's make sure we know who and what the enemy is, however, so we are not fighting the wrong enemy!

Our enemy is not flesh and blood, and we need to be careful how and what we tackle ... we are fighting spiritual forces in high places. We cannot afford to be less than fully equipped ... we must *"take on the full armor of God"* – not just part of it. Paul says that a *"day of evil comes ... "* and we must be ready!

You cannot win against Satan and evil if you

are not prepared to battle with the proper attire. Paul is clear about the importance of proper armor … basically spiritual in nature. Notice all the verbs for *"put on"* … an action on our part. Christ may make the equipment available, but we must put it on.

It would have been foolish for a soldier of Rome to go into the battlefield improperly dressed. That would have been military suicide! Sometimes we take too lightly the power of the enemy we fight and the need to be properly equipped to deal with him. Too often we joke about *"letting our guard down"* … this can be serious, a matter of spiritual life or death!

Every Item of Armor Counts!

Each piece was important, and none could be discarded!

"Belt of Truth" – this represents integrity, the first piece a soldier put on. The Word as truth is the Sword mentioned later.

The *"girdle"* or *"belt"* was a hidden undergarment that all the armor pieces fastened onto to hold them together, as well as to allow flexibility in battle. This is what integrity does in our life, hidden within, but everything hinges on it!

"Breastplate of Righteousness" – Christ's

salvation, it covers all the major organs and prevents attacks from back and forward.

Salvation covers our "past" (back) ... and our "future" (forward). No sneak attack from behind will get us, nor any attack from before us. Our life is protected by His righteousness.

"Feet fitted with the readiness that comes from the Gospel of peace" – these were hobnailed sandals worn by Roman soldiers. The nails gave them good footing on rough or sandy ground and made them sure-footed.

The Gospel gives us our sure footing on rough territory, so we won't stumble and fall.

"Shield of Faith" – this "flexible" piece of equipment can cover any angle of attack. It also was made from water-saturated leather so that flaming arrows simply go out upon impact.

Faith covers all angles of attack; even the fieriest attacks are thwarted with faith!

"Helmet of Salvation" – protects the mind, the most important part of the soldier.

Salvation protects and purifies our mind, so our thoughts remain on Christ and His kingdom, for *"as a man thinketh, so is he!"*

"Sword of the Spirit" – God's Word, the only piece of equipment mentioned here that is offensive in nature.

This is our weapon against Satan! Nothing

defeats sin and Satan more than God's Word –
NOTHING!

A Supernatural Sword

The Word of God has a supernatural edge with
which a million-dollar budget can never compete.
No soldier in his right mind would enter a battle
with a piece missing. What about us? How many
times have we fought temptation and sin without
faith, without the Word of God directing us,
without integrity, without a pure mind, etc.? If we
want to win, we must be equipped and at the ready!

Total Communication

Paul also mentions prayer ... this is communication with the commander-in-chief ... something
every soldier knows as critical in a battle situation!
Prayer is communication ... it allows us to share
our fears with God, opens us to hear from Him.
Prayer is powerful communication and will
change us!

Prayer is a critical part of spiritual warfare, as
well as uniting us together for battle. Good communication is always important. We fight more
unified when we communicate together.

The Power of the Truth

Paul now speaks about the importance of proclamation ... he asks prayer for boldness to keep proclaiming the truth despite the battle. One of our presidents once said, *"The first casualty of war is truth!"* However, we must be bold to proclaim the truth no matter how unpopular it might seem – this is part of the battle!

Pastors who give their congregations only what they want are seldom able to lead them to new heights. If Moses had listened to his congregation and appeased them, the people of Israel would have returned to Egypt and bondage. A visionary pastor is one who can shake and rattle people for the cause of Christ.

Truth is strengthened when everyone holds together for it! Paul invites them to join him in preserving and proclaiming the truth of God's Word, to be bold! Paul says that proclaiming the Gospel is EXPECTED from soldiers. Notice his words here: *"Pray that I may declare it fearlessly, as I should."*

God's Ambassadors

Paul calls himself an *"ambassador in chains."* Ambassadors speak for the king or president.

Their words are his words! They represent the power of the leader they speak for. The message is clear, we speak for God, His authority, His power, His plans, not ours! Paul does not fight alone … no sane solider would!! Yet how many Christians today have not partnered with others in their battle against sin and Satan! Paul sends Tychicus, a fellow soldier, to help them since he is in chains. We cannot fight well by ourselves … we need to work together to defeat our enemy!

Prayer Focuses God's Power

During Operation Desert Storm, the Iraqi war machine was overwhelmed by the Coalition Forces' ability to strike strategic targets with never-seen-before accuracy. Unknown to the Iraqis, the Allied Supreme Command had dropped Special Operations Forces (SOF) deep behind enemy lines. These men provided bombing coordinates for military targets and first-hand reports on the effectiveness of subsequent bombing missions. To avoid unintended targets, pinpoint bombing was often required. A soldier from a SOF unit standing on the ground would request an aircraft high overhead to drop a laser-guided missile. Using a hand-held laser, the soldier would point at the target. The missile would home in on the soldier's target for the hit. In much the same way, the prayers of Christians focus the attention of the spiritual powers on high.

We Are Each Other's Support

When we look around and see other soldiers fighting alongside us, we are encouraged and emboldened to keep fighting. We need each other! We need to be accountable to one another. We need each other's support and encouragement. We MUST NOT fight each other!

What is the object of war? To defeat the enemy and win the peace! Paul can talk about *"peace"* because we will win! Paul talks also about *"undying love"* because we can't lose! The Church is full of soldiers fighting a battle against sin and Satan ... a winnable war IF we fight with the right equipment.

The world can fight its battles for land or for style of government, but the battle we fight is far more important. It is for the soul!

Winner Takes All

Who are the winners? Those left standing when the smoke clears! *"... and after you have done everything, to stand"* (v. 13). What kind of soldier are you? Are you fighting or letting everyone else do the fighting for you? Are you properly dressed for battle?

The winners of any war are the ones left standing! The Church is at war with a real enemy. God has made available the right equipment and has empowered us to fight – to stand! It is a war we can and must win! Are you properly *"dressed to kill,"* and do you know who the real enemy is?

About Tim R. Barker

Reverend Tim R. Barker is the Superintendent of the South Texas District of the Assemblies of God which is headquartered in Houston, Texas

He is a graduate of Southwestern Assemblies of God University, with a Bachelor of Science degree in General Ministries /Biblical Studies, with a minor in music. He also received a Master of Arts in Practical Theology from SAGU and received his Doctorate of Ministry Degree from West Coast Seminary.

Reverend Barker was ordained by the Assemblies of God in 1989. He began his ministry in the South Texas District in 1984 as youth & music minister and continued his ministry as Pastor, Executive Presbyter (2006 – 2009) and Executive Secretary-Treasurer (2009 – 2011) in the South Texas District, where he served until his election as the South Texas District Superinten- dent in 2011.

By virtue of his district office, Reverend Barker is a member of the District's Executive

Presbytery and the General Presbytery of the General Council of the Assemblies of God, Springfield, Missouri. He is a member of the Executive Board of Regents for Southwestern Assemblies of God University, Waxahachie, Texas and SAGU-American Indian College, Phoenix, Arizona. He is a member of the Board of Directors of Pleasant Hills Children's Home, Fairfield, Texas, as well as numerous other boards and committees.

Reverend Barker and his wife, Jill, married in 1983, have been blessed with two daughters. Jordin and her husband, Stancle Williams, who serves as the South Texas District Youth Director. Abrielle and her husband, Nolan McLaughlin are church planters of Motion Church in San Antonio. The Barkers have four grandchildren, Braylen, Emory and Landon Williams and Kingston McLaughlin.

His unique style of pulpit ministry and musical background challenges the body of Christ, with an appeal that reaches the generations.

A Final Word

You can find Tim on the South Texas District website at www.stxag.org, on Facebook, or at his Houston office when he's not traveling his home state ministering in the churches across the South Texas District.

He'd be thrilled to connect with you and share stories of God's faithfulness.

— Notes —

— Notes —

— Notes —

— Notes —

— Notes —

— Notes —